KILLER WHALES

LIVING WILD

Published by Creative Education
P.O. Box 227, Mankato, Minnesota 56002
Creative Education is an imprint of The Creative Company
www.thecreativecompany.us

Design and production by Mary Herrmann
Art direction by Rita Marshall
Printed by Corporate Graphics in the United States of America

Photographs by 123RF (cbpix), Alamy (Arco Images GmbH, Mary Evans Picture Library, Photos 12), Corbis (Werner Forman, Norbert Wu/Science Faction), Dreamstime (George Burba, Lars Christensen, Stephen Coburn, Fredericb, Glen Gaffney, Todd Gantzler, Benjamin Gelman, Maxfx), Getty Images (Cris Bouroncle/AFP, Rick Price), iStockphoto (Frederic Borsset, Karoline Cullen, Jan Daly, James Dare, Jami Garrison, John Gaudette, Richard Goerg, Brian Gudas, Alexander Hafemann, Tatiana Ivkovich, Benjamin Jessop, Håkan Karlsson, Michael Kempf, Evgeniya Lazareva, Tomasz Szymanski)

Library of Congress Cataloging-in-Publication Data
Gish, Melissa.
Killer whales / by Melissa Gish.
p. cm. — (Living wild)
Includes bibliographical references and index.
Summary: A look at killer whales, including their habitats, physical characteristics such as their unique coloration, behaviors, relationships with humans, and protected status in the world today.
ISBN 978-1-58341-971-7
1. Killer whale—Juvenile literature. I. Title. II. Series.

QL737.C432G57 2010
599.53'6—dc22   2009025172

CPSIA: 120109 PO1092
First Edition
9 8 7 6 5 4 3 2 1

C CREATIVE EDUCATION

KILLER WHALES

Melissa Gish

A group of killer whales pauses its day's travels to gather in the chilly water

of Johnstone Strait, between Canada's
Vancouver Island and British Columbia.

A group of killer whales pauses its day's travels to gather in the chilly water of Johnstone Strait, between Canada's Vancouver Island and British Columbia. The sun shines brightly, but it doesn't warm the water above its early autumn average of 43 °F (6 °C). Some of the killer whales flop over onto their backs, gently rubbing against each other and soaking up the sunshine. Two youngsters, each weighing more than

1,500 pounds (680.4 kg), rush to a big male who is floating on his back. The youngsters let out loud squeaks, bumping the male on the face and then dashing away. He rolls onto his belly and floats patiently, allowing the youngsters to bump, rub, and flop on him. It is playtime for the young killer whales, and the adults—brothers and sisters, aunts and uncles—all relax and allow the lively youth to enjoy the calm afternoon.

WHERE IN THE WORLD THEY LIVE

The single species of killer whale is typically found in colder ocean waters around the globe. It primarily frequents the Arctic, North Atlantic, and North Pacific oceans in the Northern Hemisphere and the Southern Ocean in the Southern Hemisphere, and it is occasionally seen in warmer gulfs and other waters as well. The colored squares represent some common locations.

■ **Killer Whale**
most common in Arctic
and Southern oceans

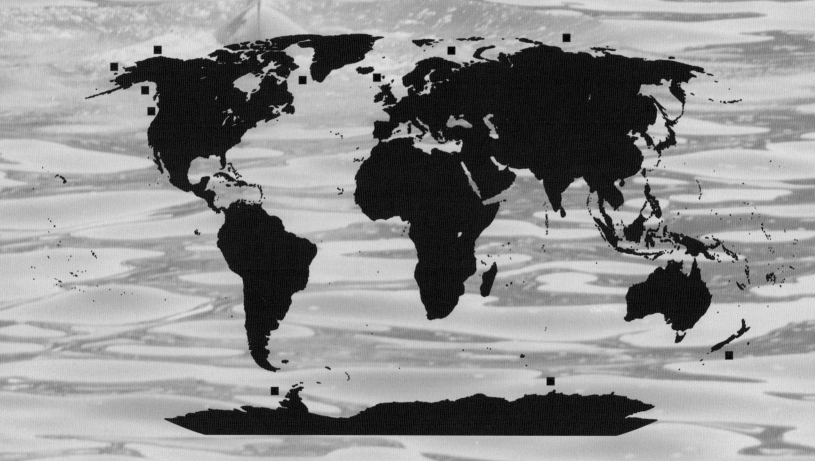

WHALE KILLERS

The killer whale is one of Earth's top predators, hunting and eating just about anything it can catch in all five of the world's oceans. Groups of killer whales will even attack the largest animals in the sea—whales. The common name "killer whale" is derived from the name *ballena asesina*, or "whale killer," which was what 18th-century sailors who saw groups of killer whales ripping apart enormous whales many times their size called the creatures. Their scientific name, *Orcinus orca*, relates to Orcus, a god of the underworld in Roman **mythology**. In Latin, *orcinus* means "from hell," and *orc* means "whale."

While killer whales are found all around the world, they are most common in the Arctic and Southern oceans. They also live off the icy Pacific coasts of Alaska and Canada, the frigid Atlantic coasts of Iceland and Norway, and in the chilly waters of the Southern Ocean near Argentina. Because most killer whales are constantly on the move in search of food, they may even venture into warm waters, such as those of the Indian Ocean and Gulf of Mexico, and up rivers such as Oregon's Columbia River.

The Etruscans, an important Mediterranean culture around 500 B.C., decorated temples with images of Orcus.

Killer whales living off the coast of Norway feed on schools of herring, and killer whales in New Zealand's waters eat sharks and stingrays.

Despite being related to killer whales, dolphins instinctively flee when the predators come too near.

A killer whale's ears cannot be seen because they are located in a foam-filled cavity between the skull and the skin, held in place by ligaments.

The killer whale is not a whale but rather the largest member of the dolphin family Delphinidae. The killer whale's closest relatives are the pygmy killer whale and the other 31 species of dolphin. Killer whales are marine mammals, meaning they live in the water and belong to a class of animals that, with the exception of the egg-laying platypus and echidnas, give birth to live young and produce milk to feed them.

Like all mammals, killer whales are warm-blooded. This means that their bodies maintain a constant temperature that is usually warmer than their surroundings. To help it stay warm, the killer whale has three to four inches (8–10 cm) of thick fat, called blubber, just beneath its skin. Blood vessels in the fluke, flippers, and dorsal fin (which is located on its back) also help the killer whale control its temperature.

Since mammals need to breathe air, killer whales must regularly swim to the surface of the water. A killer whale breathes through its blowhole, a type of nostril located on top of its head. Once it reaches the surface, the killer whale opens its blowhole, sucks in a great amount of air, and then pinches its blowhole shut as it dives into the water.

Toothed whales such as the killer whale have one blowhole, while baleen whales such as the humpback have two.

Certain killer whales are always on the move and can travel 75 to 100 miles (121–161 km) each day.

To dine on a school of fish, killer whales first smack them with their tails to knock them out or blow bubbles to force them to the surface.

Killer whales have enormous lungs that allow them to stay underwater for up to 15 minutes. Such lengthy dives are rare, however. Usually, killer whales remain underwater for no more than 5 minutes, and most of the time, they swim near the water's surface to take a breath every 30 seconds.

Killer whales are the only species of dolphin with black skin. They have distinctive white eye and belly markings that are unique to each killer whale and are used by researchers to distinguish one killer whale from another. Individuals can also be recognized by the gray or whitish mark behind the dorsal fin, called a saddle patch, which varies in shape and coloration from one killer whale to another.

Killer whales are massive creatures, nearly the length of a school bus. Females typically weigh about 8,000 pounds (3,629 kg) and grow to 16 to 23 feet (4.8–7 m) in length. The average male weighs up to 12,000 pounds (5,443 kg) and is more than 26 feet (8 m) long. Adult killer whales have more than 40 interlocking teeth. The snout is tapered, the body is smooth and sleek, and the tail is slender. This streamlined shape allows for little **resistance**

as a killer whale cuts through the water, enabling it to move at great speeds while chasing prey and to dive and surface quickly.

The tail is what gives a killer whale its speed. At the end of the tail are two flat, boneless pads called flukes. The killer whale uses the muscles in its back and tail to wave the flukes up and down. This motion propels the killer whale forward—at speeds of up to 30 miles (48 km) per hour.

To help steer as it swims, the killer whale uses its pectoral flippers. These are located on each side of the

A killer whale has 50 to 54 bones in its back but none in the fluke, which is why some flukes curl with age.

Female killer whales float on their backs so their offspring can nurse without being in danger of drowning.

chest below and behind the head. The flippers have bones similar to those in a human's hand, enabling the killer whale to twist its pectoral flippers somewhat sideways in order to slow down or stop swimming. The killer whale uses its dorsal fin to steady itself as it swims. Without the weight of this boneless appendage, a killer whale would roll upside-down in the water. A young male's or female's dorsal fin is usually three to four feet (1–1.2 m) tall and curves to the right or left. When a male reaches 12 to 14 years of age, his dorsal fin grows taller and straightens, eventually reaching up to 6 feet (1.8 m) in height.

Killer whales communicate vocally with each other by making clicks, whistles, pulsed calls, and pops. Whistles change pitch, like songs, and are used to communicate socially in groups. Pulsed calls sound like squeaks or screeches, while pops are low-frequency sounds. Pulsed calls and clicks are also used during **echolocation**.

Echolocation helps killer whales to "see" underwater. To echolocate, a killer whale sends out pulses of sound from various nasal sacs and cavities. These sounds hit objects in their path and bounce back, like echoes, and are captured by a fatty organ in the forehead called a melon. The killer whale then "reads" the echoes, determining the location, shape, and size of the objects around it—including prey. The objects can be as big as a whale or as small as a fish. With this ability, killer whales can hunt, even in total darkness. Using echolocation, killer whales can determine the differences between humans and prey animals such as seals. This is the reason, researchers believe, that killer whales do not attack humans in the ocean.

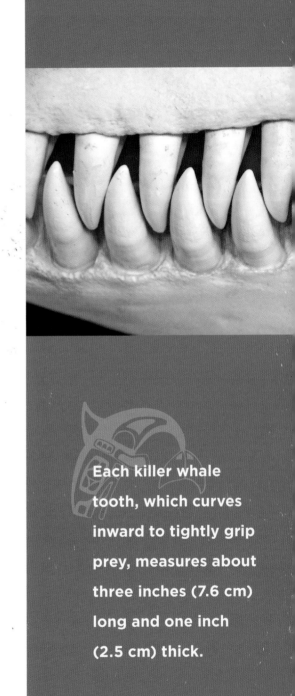

Each killer whale tooth, which curves inward to tightly grip prey, measures about three inches (7.6 cm) long and one inch (2.5 cm) thick.

When a pod of killer whales gathers together and floats on the water's surface, the action is called logging.

FAMILY MATTERS

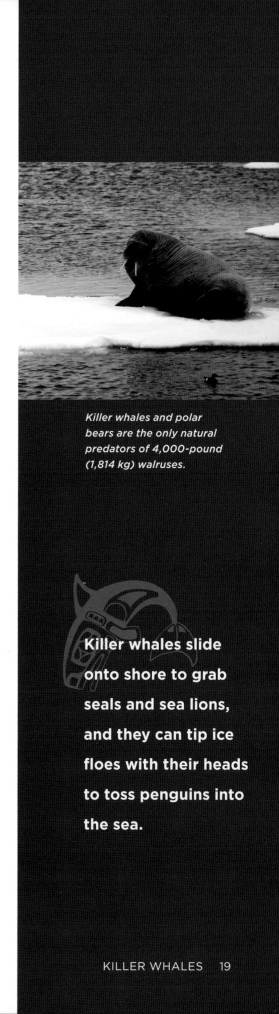

Killer whales live in family groups called pods, which are led by a dominant female known as the matriarch. A pod is made up of several mothers and their offspring and includes 10 to 20 members that travel together for their entire lives. By biting, head-butting, and scraping her teeth on other killer whales' skin, a matriarch shows her pod members that she is in charge. When she dies, one of her daughters takes over.

There are three kinds of killer whale pods: offshore, **transient**, and resident. Offshore killer whales stay far from land at all times. Little is known about their behavior, as their pods are very small, and they are not easy to find. Transients tend to hunt silently in small groups and sneak up on their favorite prey, including seals, sea lions, walruses, and dolphins. Individual transients may move from pod to pod throughout their lives. Offshore and transient killer whales **migrate** in summer and winter to follow stocks of fish that also migrate. Residents tend to stay in the same pods their entire lives. They do not migrate over long distances but instead travel around a specific range. They eat smaller

Killer whales and polar bears are the only natural predators of 4,000-pound (1,814 kg) walruses.

Killer whales slide onto shore to grab seals and sea lions, and they can tip ice floes with their heads to toss penguins into the sea.

Killer whales are able to sneak up on unsuspecting seals or penguins, even in the midst of ice-filled waters.

prey, passing up seals in favor of fish, and they spend a great deal of time vocally communicating with members of their pod.

Body language is another important form of communication. When a killer whale propels itself out of the water quickly and falls back down with a big splash, it is breaching. This is one way it shows off its strength. To show dominance, a killer whale might loudly smack its tail or paddle its flippers on the water's surface. In addition to such displays, killer whales utilize many other kinds of signals to tell each other where food is located or where danger is lurking.

Pod members stay close together. Many pods that live near each other can be classified as a clan. The killer whales of a clan are all related to one another. Because killer whales will not mate with relatives, several clans will gather together in a community of 100 or more individuals that are not all related to facilitate mating. Resident communities will mate and then separate, but clans of transient and offshore communities, also known as superpods, may travel and hunt together in addition to mating.

Mating occurs only during specific seasons, which vary depending on the climate in which the pod lives. Summer is the most common time for killer whale mating to take place. Female killer whales mature when they are about 15 feet (4.6 m) long, which could happen any time between the ages of 6 and 10 years. A female will breed once every 3 to 10 years until she is 40 years old. Males mature when they are about 20 feet (6.1 m) long and their dorsal fins have reached full height. This happens when the males are about 12 to 14 years old.

The first thing that a female notices about a potential mate is the dorsal fin. Females are usually most attracted to older males whose dorsal fins are very tall. When a female decides to pay attention to a male, she will watch him slap the surface of the water with his flippers and flukes. Then the male will chase the female around, splashing and bumping her body with his head and body. He will swim close to her, rubbing his skin against hers. If she likes him, she will invite him to mate with her.

Killer whales mate while swimming together. A female will mate with several males to increase her chances of producing strong offspring. After mating, the community breaks up into smaller clans or pods. Because the fathers move back to their own pods, they take no part in the **rearing** of their offspring, called calves. Males

Born ready to swim, a calf quickly learns from its mother all it needs to know about survival in the sea.

The killer whale has a sleek, streamlined body that is tapered at both ends, a shape described as fusiform.

in a calf's pod—its brothers and uncles—will protect and teach it throughout its early years.

The female carries her single calf for 15 to 17 months; twins are rare. When the calf is ready to be born, the mother swims in a twisting, rolling motion to help push out the calf, which emerges tail first. Instinct drives the newborn calf toward the water's surface. The mother lifts the calf with her snout to help it take its first breath.

Newborn calves are seven to nine feet (2.1–2.7 m) long. They can weigh up to 400 pounds (181 kg). For the first few days of its life, a calf's flippers and flukes are floppy. And for the first year, a calf's light-colored areas of skin are creamy instead of white.

The milk produced by a female killer whale is full of

the fat and nutrients that her calf needs to grow. The calf presses its mouth against its mother's body, and she squirts milk directly into its mouth. At about 12 weeks, the calf's upper teeth emerge, and about 4 weeks after that, the lower teeth begin to grow. The calf then begins to eat prey with other members of its pod, but it also continues to rely on its mother's milk until it is one year old. By that time, the calf has gained about 1,000 pounds (454 kg).

A killer whale calf's life is filled with danger. It is vulnerable to attack by predators such as sharks, many of which can be twice as long as a killer whale calf. About half of all young killer whales die within the first year. Many perish at birth because they are not big enough or strong enough to survive in the sea. Predators, disease, and other factors claim the rest.

Killer whales that are related to one another help to care for calves, teaching them how to hunt, recognize danger, and communicate. Young killer whales learn vocal communication and body language by mimicking the older killer whales in the pod. Each pod has its own vocal language variation, or dialect, that is passed down from the older killer whales to the calves.

Blacktip reef sharks are a favorite target of adult killer whales.

Large sharks prey on young killer whales, but the roles reverse when the killer whales become adults and can attack the sharks.

Killer whales are kept in captivity around the world, from France's Marineland to Venezuela's Acuario Mundo Marino.

STAR OF THE SHOW

T oday, people understand that killer whales are highly intelligent and trainable, but this was not always the case. The ancient Greeks viewed killer whales as monsters bent on bringing bad luck to sailors. Common dolphins represented good luck, and seeing killer whales attack and devour dolphins struck fear and superstition into the hearts of Greek sailors, whose experiences were the basis of myths and legends surrounding killer whales.

The first written account of killer whales was published in *Natural History*, an encyclopedia written by Pliny the Elder, an ancient Roman naturalist and author, in A.D. 77. He noted the animals' "savage teeth" and described their attacks on great whales with battle imagery, saying that killer whales "charge and pierce [the great whales] like warships ramming." Such stories of monstrous "orcs" persisted for many centuries, from Italy to Sweden. In his 1555 *History of the Northern Peoples*, Swedish writer Olaus Magnus wrote how killer whales used their "ferocious teeth . . . as brigantines [fast sailing ships] do their prows [the pointed front parts of ships]" to rip into the body of a great whale.

Pliny the Elder (pictured) took much of the biological information for his Natural History *from the Greek thinker Aristotle.*

Crumbling wrecks are all that remain of the wooden whaling ships that were used into the early 20th century.

In the 19th and 20th centuries, when scientists began traveling with sailors and whalers on their voyages, the accounts of killer whales became more scientifically accurate. People began to understand that killer whales were intelligent animals, and organizations in Canada, the United States, and some northern European nations established research projects aimed at learning more about killer whales.

But just as the first observations of killer whale intelligence were being published, the whaling industry began to see the financial value of capturing killer whales. By the early 1900s, stocks of regularly hunted whales, such as fin whales and right whales, had declined drastically due to overhunting. Because killer whales were abundant, whalers turned their attention to these creatures instead. Although almost 10,000 were killed before whaling ceased in most countries in the 1980s, killer whales were spared from having to face **extinction**.

Killer whales are still **subsistence**-hunted by certain native peoples of the Arctic. For thousands of years, these cultures have valued the killer whale not only as a food source but also as a cultural icon. Some of the cultures

Early Arctic peoples often created natural memorials from bones to thank the spirits for a successful whale hunt.

Scientists are now studying the effects of chlorinated water on killer whales and other captive marine animals.

that have made the killer whale a major part of their mythologies include Native Alaskan tribes such as the Aleut, Chugach, and Inuit; the Tlingit (*KLING-git*), Kwakwaka'wakw (*KWALK-walk-ya-WALK-wuh*), Haida, and Nootka peoples of British Columbia; and the Yupik of Russia.

One belief that is shared by many native cultures is that killer whales can come ashore and transform into humans, and humans can go underwater and become killer whales. In Haida tradition, killer whales are believed to have an underwater society similar to that of humans. Likewise, Kwakwaka'wakw mythology tells that killer whales are commanded by the powerful chief of an underwater kingdom, and they must be respected.

Today, killer whales are kept in captivity for research and enjoyment. The first killer whale to be captured was named Moby Doll—although *she* was later determined to be a *he*. In 1964, Moby Doll was shot with a harpoon, which is a large barbed spear attached to a rope, at Saturna Island in British Columbia and dragged to shore to be used as an artist's model for a sculpture. The killer whale was kept in a cage and fed fish by his captors in

The pygmy killer whale, though smaller than the killer whale, is much more aggressive and incapable of being trained in captivity.

Captive killer whales have been known to express behaviors suggesting that they form bonds with their trainers.

the first recorded experience of a killer whale accepting food directly from a human's hand. Moby Doll died 87 days after his capture, but his intelligent behavior sparked people's interest in working with killer whales.

In 1965, a 10,000-pound (4,536 kg) killer whale became entangled in a fishing net off the coast of British

Columbia and was sold by its captors. Given the name Namu, the killer whale became the first of its kind to be put on public display and develop a relationship with a human. The human was Ted Griffin, owner of the Seattle Public Aquarium (now known as the Seattle Aquarium) in Washington state. After studying Namu for a month, Griffin determined that he would be safe swimming with the killer whale. He then became the first person to climb into a pool with a killer whale, and for the next 11 months, thousands of people visited the aquarium to see Namu and Griffin.

Namu was joined in Seattle by a young killer whale that had been orphaned when her mother was harpooned. The young female was afraid of Namu, so she was sent to SeaWorld in San Diego, California, where she was named Shamu. This original Shamu died after six years, in 1971. SeaWorld has since continued to showcase a killer whale named Shamu, and many zoos and aquariums around the world feature trained killer whales that perform tricks for spectators.

The oldest killer whale in captivity is Lolita, a performing killer whale housed at the Miami Seaquarium in Florida.

In 1985, Kalina became the first killer whale born in captivity to survive more than a few days; she lives at SeaWorld in Florida.

Willy the killer whale (Keiko) and Jesse (actor Jason James Richter) become best friends in the movie Free Willy.

She was captured in 1970 when she was about 3 years old and has lived at the aquarium for more than 35 years. Lolita, along with many other killer whales in captivity, is the object of a freedom campaign. People regularly write to zoo and aquarium officials and government leaders, demanding that killer whales in captivity be released back into the wild.

One killer whale that won his freedom from captivity was Keiko. He was captured near Iceland and trained to perform with humans. After Keiko starred in the 1993 film *Free Willy*, public pressure forced his captors to return Keiko to his family in the ocean. Unfortunately, Keiko had lost the ability to hunt for himself by that time, so researchers who monitored him in the wild had to provide food for him until he died of pneumonia in 2003.

The treatment of killer whales in captivity has long been a subject of public debate. Many people believe that these animals should not be forced to perform tricks for audiences and argue that no containment facility can provide the social interaction or space that killer whales enjoy in the wild. In the ocean, killer whales can live almost as long as humans, but few captive killer whales live more than 25 years.

Canto 8 of ORLANDO FURIOSO

ARGUMENT

Rogero flies; Astolpho with the rest,
To their true shape Melissa does restore;
Rinaldo levies knights and squadrons, pressed
In aid of Charles assaulted by the Moor:
Angelica, by ruffians found at rest,
Is offered to a monster on the shore.
Orlando, warned in visions of his ill,
Departs from Paris sore against his will.

LI

It here behoves me, from the path I pressed,
To turn awhile, ere I this case relate:
In the great northern sea, towards the west,
Green Ireland past, an isle is situate.
Ebuda is its name, whose shores infest,
(Its people wasted through the Godhead's hate)
The hideous orc, and Proteus' other herd,
By him against that race in vengeance stirred.

LIV

Sea-Proteus to his flocks' wide charge preferred
By Neptune, of all ocean's rule possessed,
Inflamed with ire, his lady's torment heard,
And, against law and usage, to molest
The land (no sluggard in his anger) stirred

His monsters, orc and sea-calf, with the rest;
Who waste not only herds, but human haunts,
Farm-house and town, with their inhabitants:

LVII

And this it was the cruel usage bred;
That of the damsels held most fair of face,
To Proteus every day should one be led.
Till one should in the Godhead's sight find grace.
The first and all those others slain, who fed,
All a devouring orc, that kept his place
Beside the port, what time into the main
The remnant of the herd retired again.

LXV

But such her matchless beauty's power, the maid
Was able that fierce crew to mollify,
Who many days her cruel death delayed,
Preserved until their last necessity;
And while they damsels from without purveyed,
Spared such angelic beauty: finally,
The damsel to the monstrous orc they bring,
The people all behind her sorrowing.

excerpts from Canto 8 of Orlando Furioso,
by Ludovico Ariosto (1474–1533),
translated by William Stewart Rose (1775-1843)

Wind erosion in Egypt has uncovered a treasure trove of fossilized marine mammals at least 40 million years old.

RULERS OF THE SEA

Millions of years ago, killer whale ancestors lived on land. The killer whale likely **evolved** from four-legged mammals that lived in and around streams and shallow lakes and ate plants. One killer whale ancestor was the cat-sized *Indohyus*, which lived about 50 million years ago and looked like a miniature deer. It had a thick hide like modern wading animals, such as the hippopotamus, and dense fur like that of a beaver.

As these prehistoric mammals began to spend more time in the water, they lost their legs, gaining webbed limbs and eventually flippers instead. Over many millions of years, these prehistoric creatures grew very large, out-competing any other predators. They gradually became more torpedo-shaped and developed a dorsal fin. Fossil research indicates that primitive killer whales even began to develop the ability to echolocate 10 million years ago.

The use of echolocation to hunt prey is the subject of much current killer whale research. One ongoing project that studies the relationship between killer whales and a coastal fish called herring has been conducted by the Norwegian Killer Whale Project (NORCA) since 1987.

Fossils of early whales with limbs, fingers, and toes suggest that the hippopotamus is the closest land-dwelling relative of the killer whale.

When a killer whale pops straight out of the water and then silently slips back down, it is spyhopping—checking out the surface for prey.

As herring migrate, killer whales follow to feed on them. Information on the whales and their favorite source of prey is collected using photo-identification research— taking photographs of surfacing killer whales and keeping records of the sightings—and by **satellite** tracking.

Tags are attached to the killer whales' dorsal fins or flukes. These tags have **Global Positioning System** (GPS) tracking devices on them. The information gathered from the GPS devices helps researchers count pod and clan populations, understand how and where the killer whales travel during the seasons, and learn about killer whale diving and hunting behaviors. Resident pods are the easiest to monitor, as they typically stay in the same area. Transient pods are more difficult to study, as their range is much greater. Offshore pods are generally not studied, since they are nearly impossible to find and track.

Many countries have launched research projects specifically devoted to killer whales. The Far East Russia Orca Project is the only killer whale research project in Russian waters. Scientists study the animals off the Kamchatka Peninsula in the northern Pacific Ocean. The Orca Network, an organization in Washington state, aims to provide information that will lead to the conservation of killer whales and their habitats. It sponsors research on the impacts that habitat damage, industrial pollution, and other human activities can have on killer whale populations.

Another Washington-based research project monitors a pod of resident killer whales and has noted a steady decline in the pod's population. While killer whales have long been protected from hunting by the Marine Mammal Protection Act of 1972, other human factors, such as pollution from industry and shipping traffic and overfishing of key prey, are known to affect killer whales. Additionally, when people expand cities by developing areas near killer whale habitat, the ocean resources on which killer whales depend are affected.

Researchers around the world have formed networks through which they share information on killer whales— generally by means of photo-identification research. The Orca Research Trust, founded by Dr. Ingrid Visser, is an organization that gathers information from researchers in the South Pacific, and Dr. Visser's Antarctic Killer Whale Identification Catalogue is a collaborative project that

Whale watching is a popular activity, with about 13 million people in 19 countries taking to the sea annually.

Killer whales in frigid Antarctic waters hunt the largest fish available—the six-foot (1.8 m) Antarctic cod.

gathers and shares photos of individual killer whales in the Southern Ocean.

Scientists at such places as the North Gulf Oceanic Society in Alaska and the Vancouver Aquarium Marine Science Centre in British Columbia rely on photo-identification research to monitor the health of killer whale populations. They also take **DNA** samples by shooting small darts into the bodies of killer whales, which harmlessly extract tiny samples of skin and blubber. Scientists can then analyze the **genes** of killer whales to study how female killer whales are able to determine which potential mates are not relatives.

With the tissue samples, scientists can also identify the types and amounts of **contaminants** in the killer whales' bodies. Some common contaminants are DDT and PCBs. DDT is a chemical used to kill pests on crops. It has a history of washing into waterways, where it is consumed by animals, negatively affecting them in various ways. PCBs are industrial chemicals that also find their way into Earth's water sources, and when consumed, they cause long-term damage to organs such as the liver and stomach.

Other environmental studies focus on the effect of **global warming** on killer whales. As ocean temperatures rise, fewer **plankton** survive, resulting in less food for fish—which means less food for killer whales. Environmental changes that influence a top ocean predator such as the killer whale may negatively affect every other life form on the **food chain**.

Killer whale behavior is also a subject of research. Because killer whales are highly social animals with complex communication techniques, they are easily disturbed by unnatural activities. Noise caused by industry, military activities (such as sonar testing and underwater explosions), and tourism can disrupt killer whales'

In recent decades, North Atlantic killer whales have learned to follow fishing vessels to eat discarded herring.

Killer whales may survive colliding with ships or being cut by propellers, but most that become trapped in commercial fishing gear drown.

The millions of sonar bursts emitted annually from submarines have harmful effects on whales, dolphins, and killer whales.

communication and hunting behaviors. Loud noises in the water can cause killer whales to become confused or separated from their pods, or they may accidentally swim too close to shore and get stuck on the beach.

The types of noises that affect killer whales and the sounds that killer whales make are studied using cameras and audio recording devices. The information gained from such methods helps researchers learn about the role of vocal communication and echolocation on killer whale social structure, pod movement, and hunting behaviors. For example, it has been learned that killer whales call to each other using sound variations that identify individuals—much like calling one another by name.

Being ocean-dwelling animals, killer whales are difficult to study. Enough has been learned about them, though, to dispel the many misconceptions about these brainy social creatures. No longer viewed as monsters of the deep, killer whales are now referred to as "sea pandas," fascinating animals with great intelligence and charm. Protecting their habitat—Earth's oceans—is integral to keeping killer whales alive and sustaining a balanced food chain in the seas.

Because breathing is not instinctive to killer whales, they shut down only one side of their brain at a time to sleep.

ANIMAL TALE: NATCITLANEH CREATES THE KILLER WHALE

Tlingit culture is tied to the icy ocean and its creatures. The native people of Canada's Pacific coast believe that all things were created for a reason and that people and animals share a special relationship based on respect. The following Tlingit story explains how the killer whale, called "Teek" in the Tlingit language, came to be and why people should respect rather than fear it.

Long ago, there was a skilled sea lion hunter named Natcitlaneh. He met

and fell in love with the daughter of a neighboring chief, who gave Natcitlaneh permission to marry her. Natcitlaneh moved to the chief's village and married his daughter. He proved his worth by hunting many sea lions and providing a bounty for the village. This made his new wife's brothers jealous.

One day, the brothers invited Natcitlaneh to join them in hunting sea lions on the ice floes far from shore. They all climbed into their canoes and headed out to sea. When Natcitlaneh could no longer see the shore, the

brothers tipped his canoe and sent him tumbling into the icy water. Then they took his canoe and left him floundering in the sea.

The sea lions, respecting his skill as a hunter, rescued Natcitlaneh and took him to their village in the ice caves of a glacier. The sea lions' chief was sick, but Natcitlaneh healed him. This pleased the sea lions, who then gave Natcitlaneh a magical knife. With the knife, they told him, he could carve a magnificent new animal that would carry him home.

The sea lions took Natcitlaneh to a dense forest on a nearby island, where he cut down a yellow cedar tree and began to carve with his magical knife. He carved a great fishlike creature with broad flippers, a tall dorsal fin, a strong tail, and mighty jaws. When he placed the carving in the sea, it came to life.

Natcitlaneh climbed on the killer whale's back and rode it across the sea toward his wife and their village. As they traveled, Natcitlaneh told the killer whale the story of how his brothers-in-law had betrayed him and left him to die.

As they approached the shore, Natcitlaneh saw his brothers-in-law in their canoes. They were going to hunt sea lions. Before Natcitlaneh could stop the killer whale, the great beast swam to the canoes and smashed them with its tail. The brothers-in-law fell into the water, thrashing and crying out. The killer whale was so angry at the men's betrayal of Natcitlaneh that it leaped on them, crushing their canoes and drowning them.

Natcitlaneh was avenged, but he felt regret for allowing his wife's brothers to be killed. He made the killer whale promise that it would never again harm a human being. The killer whale promised, and then it returned to the sea. It swam in circles back and forth along the shore, ever watchful over Natcitlaneh, but it never hurt anyone again.

The people of the village were amazed by Natcitlaneh's story, and when they saw for themselves that the killer whale had kept its promise, they took the honorable killer whale as their village symbol. And to this day, killer whales never, ever eat humans.

GLOSSARY

contaminants – non-natural substances that have a negative effect upon the environment or animals

DNA – deoxyribonucleic acid; a substance found in every living thing that determines the species and individual characteristics of that thing

echolocation – a system used by some animals to locate and identify objects by emitting high-pitched sounds that reflect off the object and return to the animal's ears or other sensory organs

evolved – gradually developed into a new form

extinction – the act or process of becoming extinct; coming to an end or dying out

food chain – a system in nature in which living things are dependent on each other for food

genes – the basic physical units of heredity

Global Positioning System – a system of satellites, computers, and other electronic devices that work together to determine the location of objects or living things that carry a trackable device

global warming – the gradual increase in Earth's temperature that causes changes in climates, or long-term weather conditions, around the world

ligaments – bands of tough, flexible tissue that connect bones and hold organs in place inside the body

migrate – to travel from one region or climate to another for feeding or breeding purposes

mythology – a collection of myths, or popular, traditional beliefs or stories that explain how something came to be or that are associated with a person or object

plankton – microscopic algae and animals that drift or float in the ocean

rearing – bringing up and caring for a child or young animal until it is fully grown

resistance – the slowing effect applied by one thing against another

satellite – a mechanical device launched into space; it may be designed to travel around Earth or toward other planets or the sun

subsistence – relating to production of something at a small-scale level, without extra to trade

transient – staying in a place for only a short time

SELECTED BIBLIOGRAPHY

American Cetacean Society. "Orca (Killer Whale)." ACS Online. http://acsonline.org/factpack/KillerWhale.htm.

Getten, Mary J. *Communicating with Orcas: The Whales' Perspective.* Charlottesville, Va.: Hampton Roads Publishing, 2006.

Hoyt, Erich. *Orca: The Whale Called Killer.* Rochester, N.Y.: Camden House, 1990.

MarineBio Society. "*Orcinus orca*, Orca (Killer Whale)." MarineBio.org. http://marinebio.org/species.asp?id=84.

Morton, Alexandra. *Listening to Whales: What the Orcas Have Taught Us.* New York: Ballantine Books, 2002.

Orca Network. "Homepage." http://www.orcanetwork.org.

Killer whales may breach to get rid of dead skin, as their skin cells grow 290 times faster than those on a human arm.

INDEX